Discovering PIANO LITERATURE

35 Carefully Graded Original Early Intermediate Piano Solos from the Four Stylistic Periods

---

NOTE TO THE TEACHER

Discover the world of piano literature with this collection of early intermediate piano solos. You and your students will enjoy discovering some less familiar pieces, while gaining new insights into favorite masterworks.

The selections in *Discovering Piano Literature* represent the four style periods and include a newly commissioned piece. All of the pieces are in their original form. The pieces are arranged in approximate order of difficulty within each style period.

In the table of contents, theoretical elements are listed to quicken your evaluation and presentation of each piece. Teaching theory contained in the music is an efficient use of lesson time and reinforces the strong connection between understanding music theory and understanding each new piece. If the student views a new piece as disorganized dots on the page, this view negatively affects the learning and the ultimate performance.

The literature contained in *Discovering Piano Literature* is approximately the same level as the music in the *First Impressions* Music and Study Guides:

Use *Discovering Piano Literature* Book 1 with *First Impressions* Volume A and B

Use *Discovering Piano Literature* Book 2 with *First Impressions* Volume C and 1

Use *Discovering Piano Literature* Book 3 with *First Impressions* Volume 2 and 3

Book 1 of *Discovering Piano Literature* can be introduced at about the same time the student begins Book 3 of *Alfred's Basic Piano Library.* The book provides excellent supplementary material for any method.

Cover art: Planet Art

Selected and Edited by M'lou Dietzer

TABLE OF CONTENTS

Listed by style periods; theoretical and technical elements featured in each piece are listed below.

*Commissioned by M'lou Dietzer

DANCE

Daniel Gottlob Türk
(1750–1813)

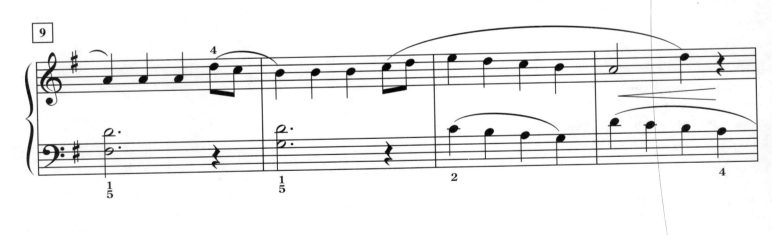

Gavotte

James Hook
(1746–1827)

Prelude

Daniel Gottlob Türk
(1750–1813)

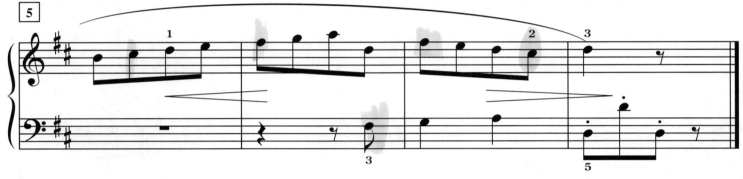

Court Dance

Daniel Gottlob Türk
(1750–1813)

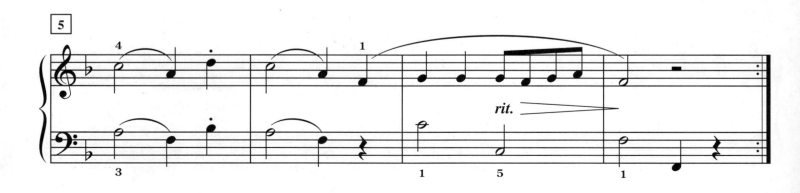

ENTRADA

Michael Praetorius
(1571–1621)

GAVOTTE

Georg Philipp Telemann
(1681–1767)

CORRENTE

Daniel Gottlob Türk
(1750–1813)

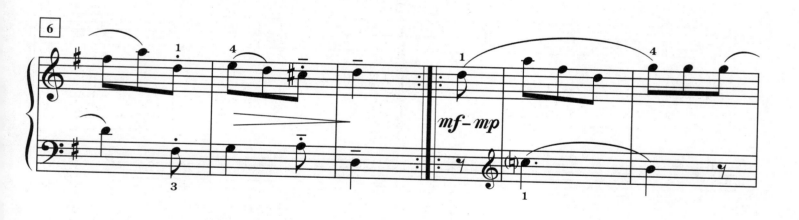

Minuet

Johann Krieger
(1651–1735)

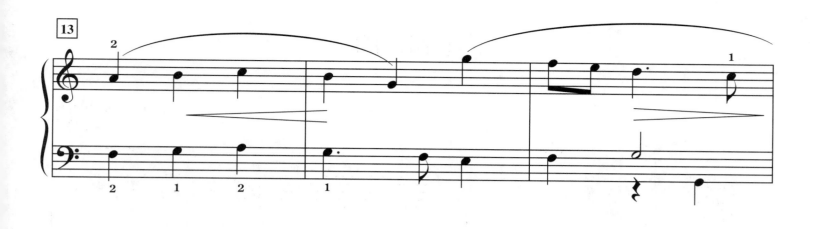

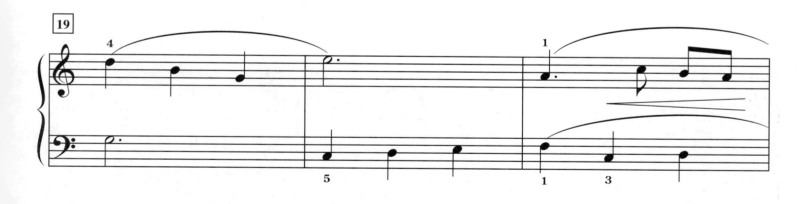

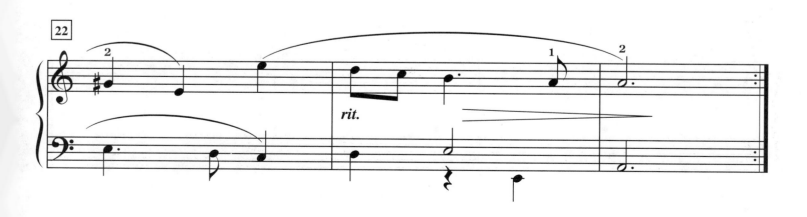

Gavotte

Benjamin Carr
(1768–1831)

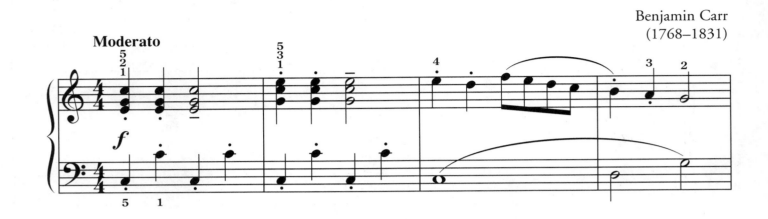

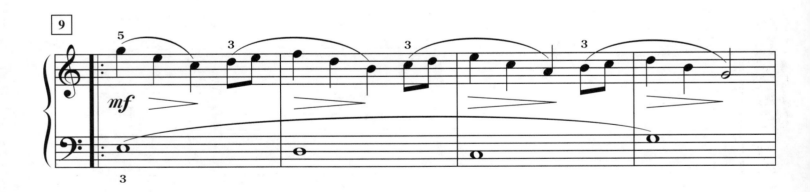

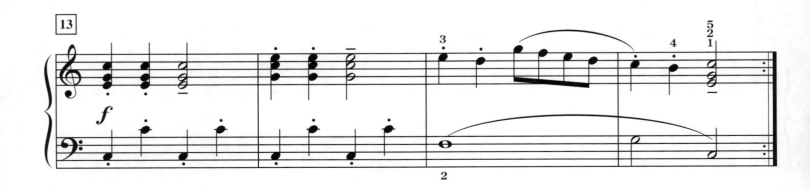

Minuet

Anton Diabelli
(1781–1858)

Quadrille

Franz Joseph Haydn
(1732–1809)

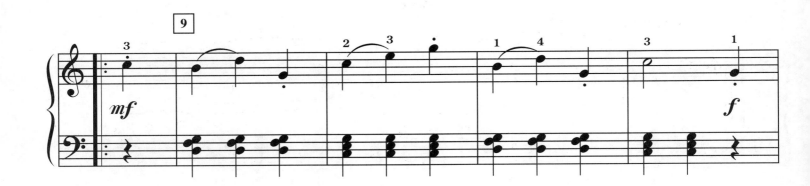

TWO BAGATELLES

I.

Jan Jakub Ryba
(1765–1815)

II.

Ecossaise

Johann Nepomuk Hummel
(1778–1837)

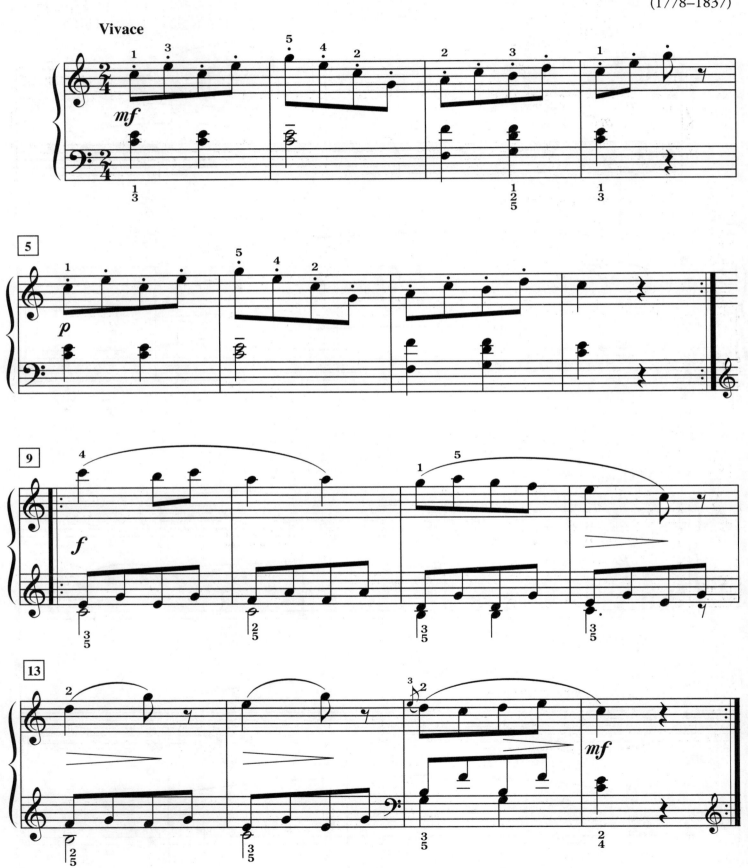

Nannerl's Minuet

Leopold Mozart
(1719–1787)

SONATINA

Tobias Haslinger
(1787–1842)

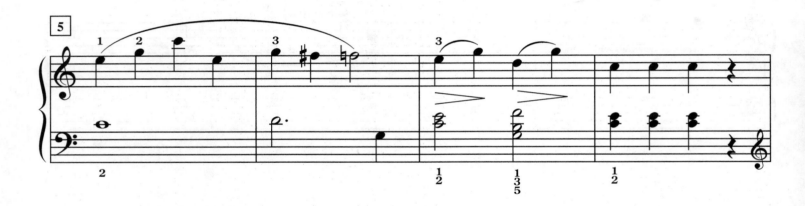

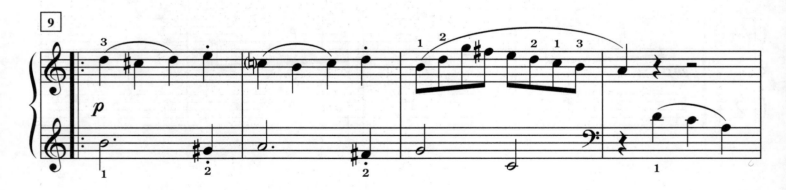

Bourrée

Wolfgang Amadeus Mozart
(1756–1791)

COUNTRY DANCE

Heinrich Wohlfahrt
(1797–1883)

WALTZ

Emil Breslaur
(1836–1899)

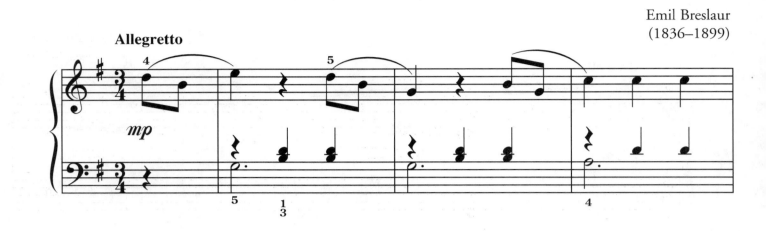

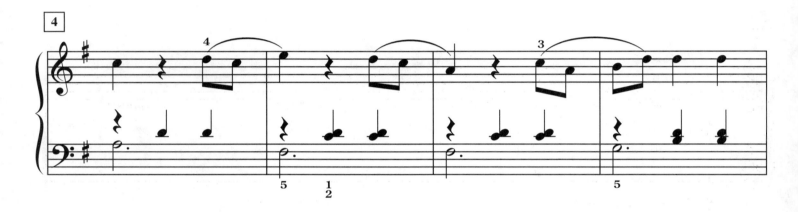

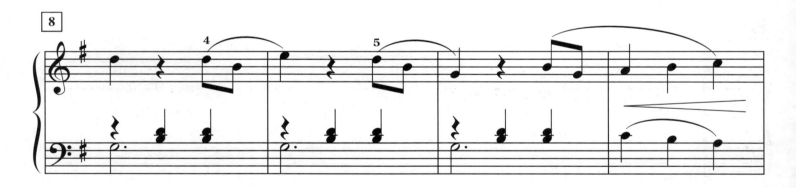

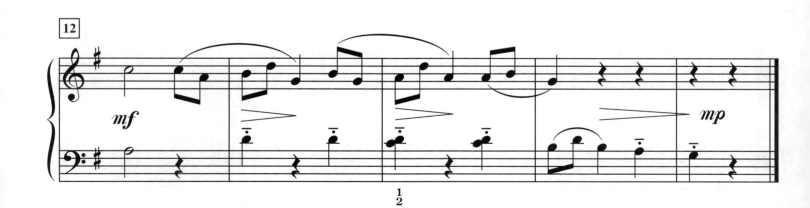

CELEBRATION

Cornelius Gurlitt
(1820–1901)

CONVERSATION

Arnoldo Sartorio
b. 1853

SERIOUS THOUGHTS

V. Gerstein
(dates unknown)

The Cuckoo

Eduard Horák
(1839–1892)

GARDEN PARTY

Jean-Louis Streabbog
(1835–1886)

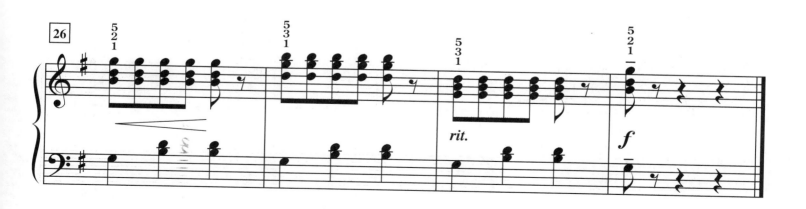

SCHERZO

Cornelius Gurlitt
(1820–1901)

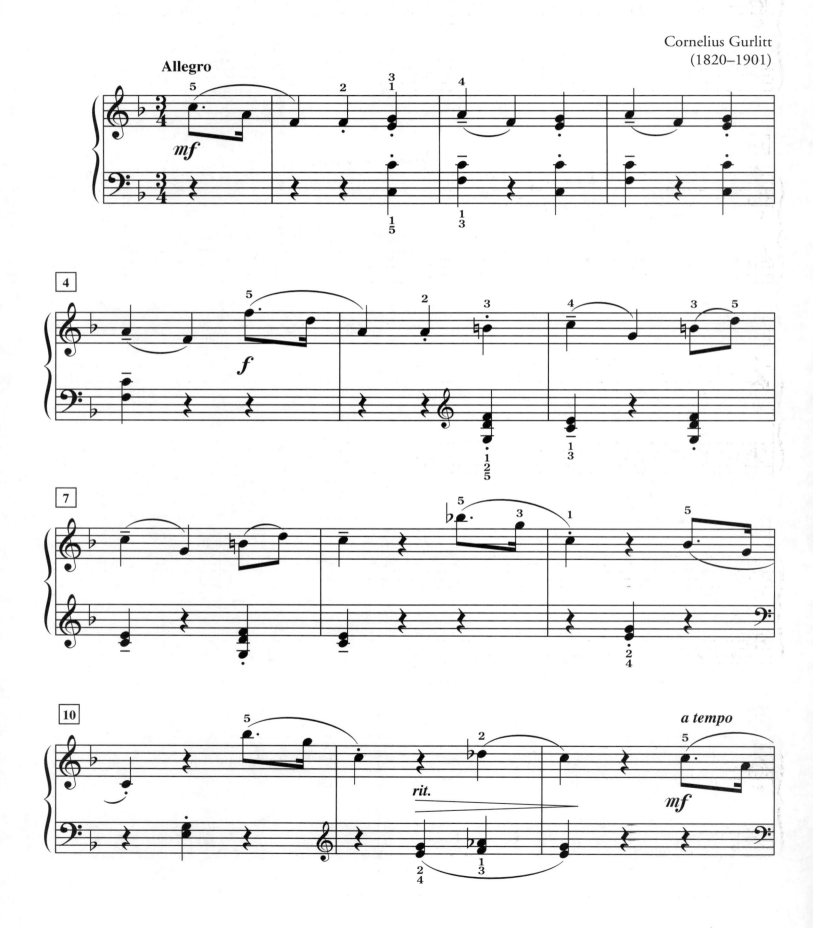

A Summer Day

Jean Baptiste Duvernoy
(1802–1880)

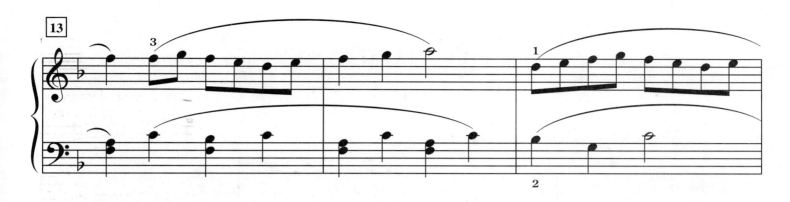

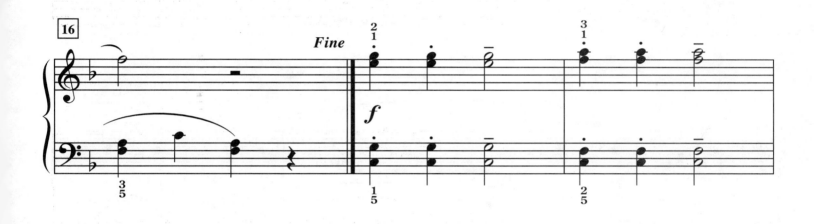

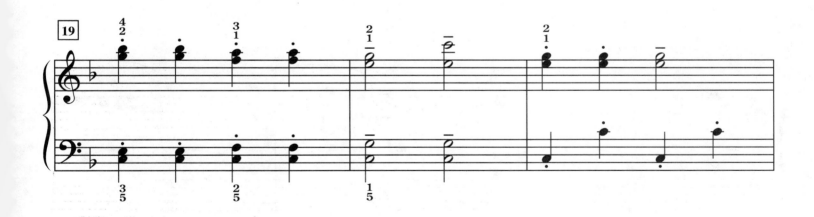

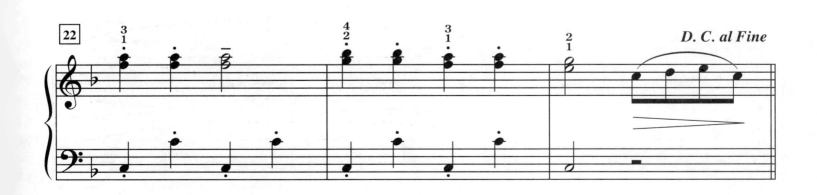

Melody

Felix Le Couppey
(1811–1887)

THE DANCING LESSON

Arnoldo Sartorio
b. 1853

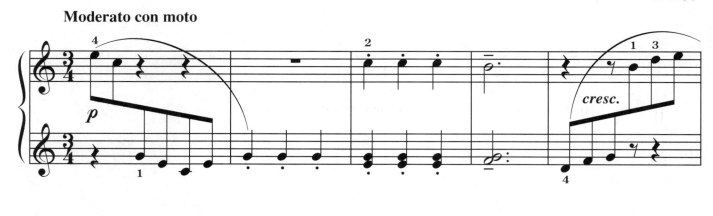

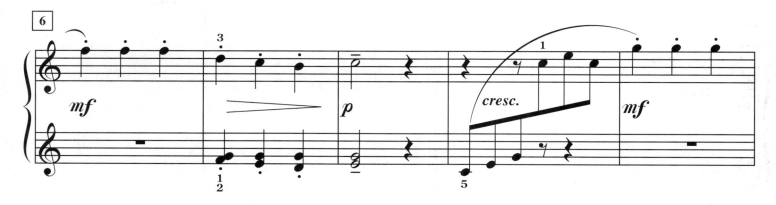

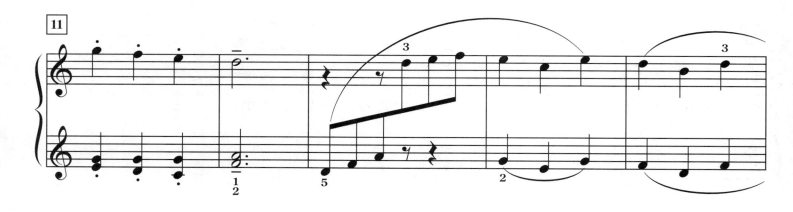

BICYCLE RACE

Lemoine
(dates unknown)

A Quiet Moment

Béla Bartók
(1881–1945)

THE SHEPHERD'S FLUTE

Tat'iana Salutrinskaya
(dates unknown)

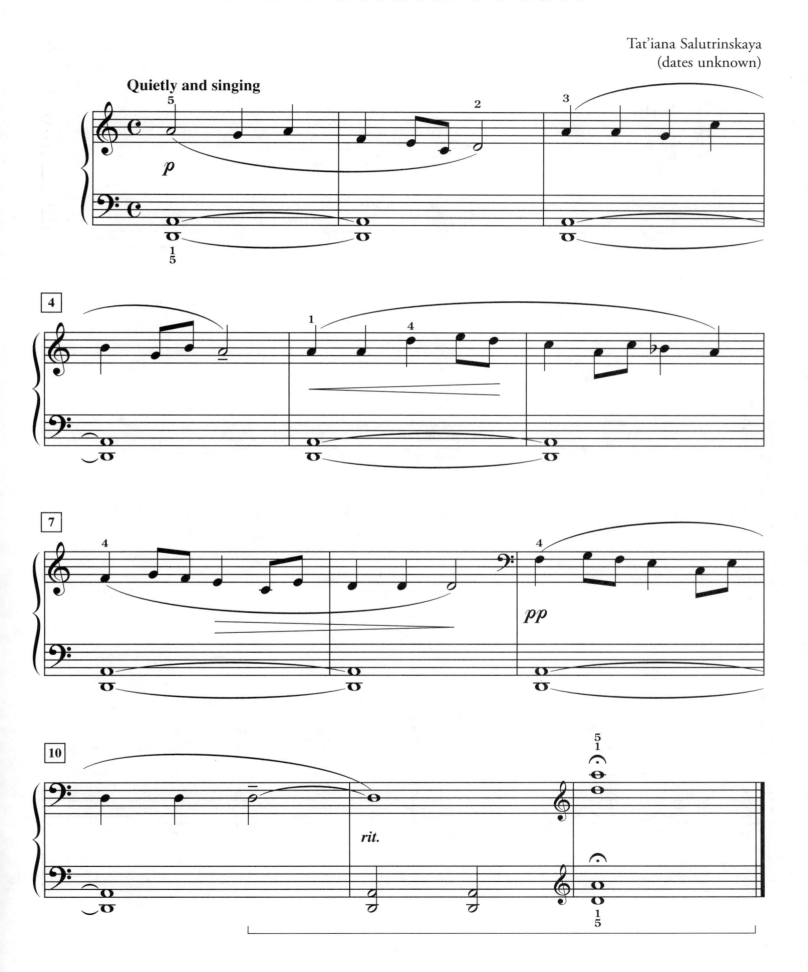

FROGS

Mary Ann Parker
(1936–)

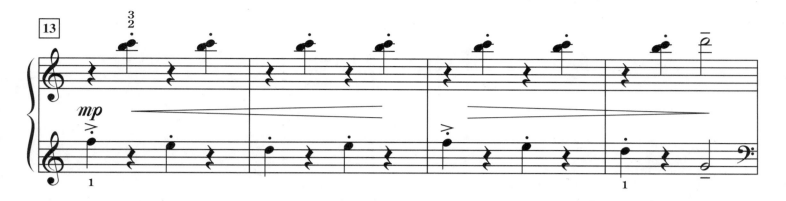

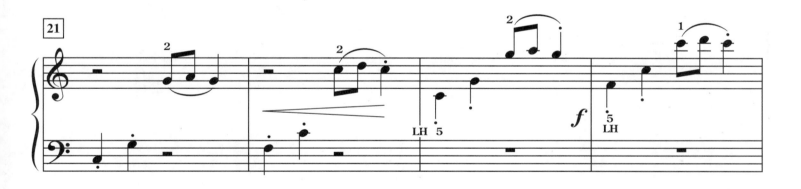

Springtime

Béla Bartók
(1881–1945)

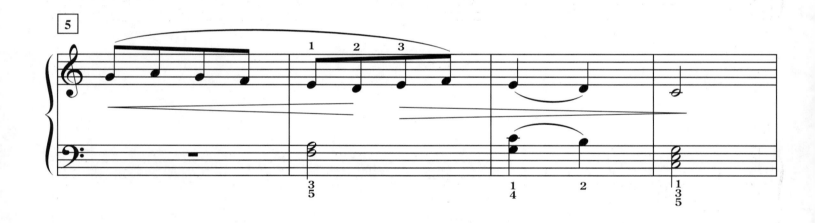

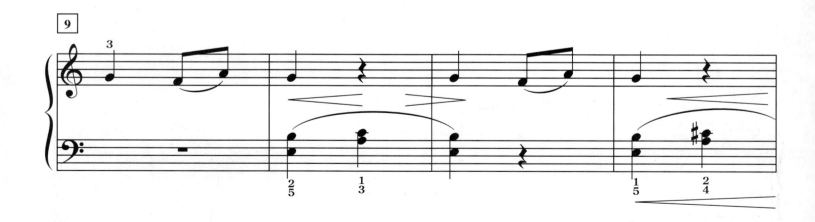

Playing Soldiers

Vladimir Rebikov
(1866–1920)

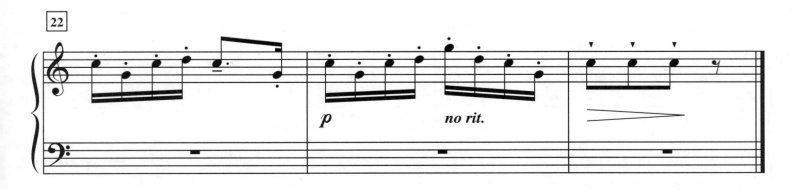

CHILDREN AT PLAY

Béla Bartók
(1881–1945)

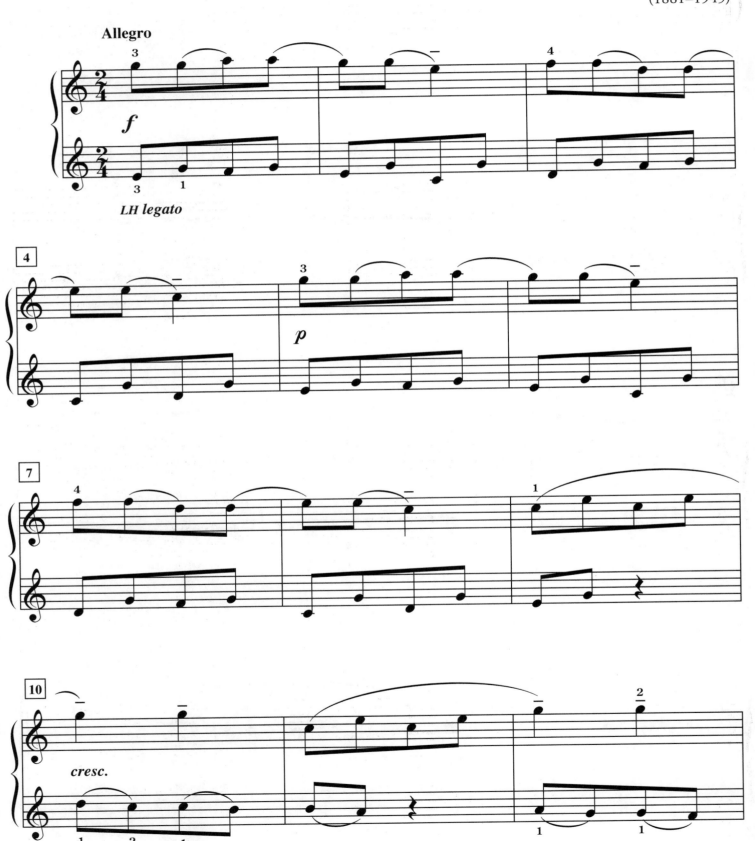

As Darkness Falls...

M'lou Dietzer
(1929–)

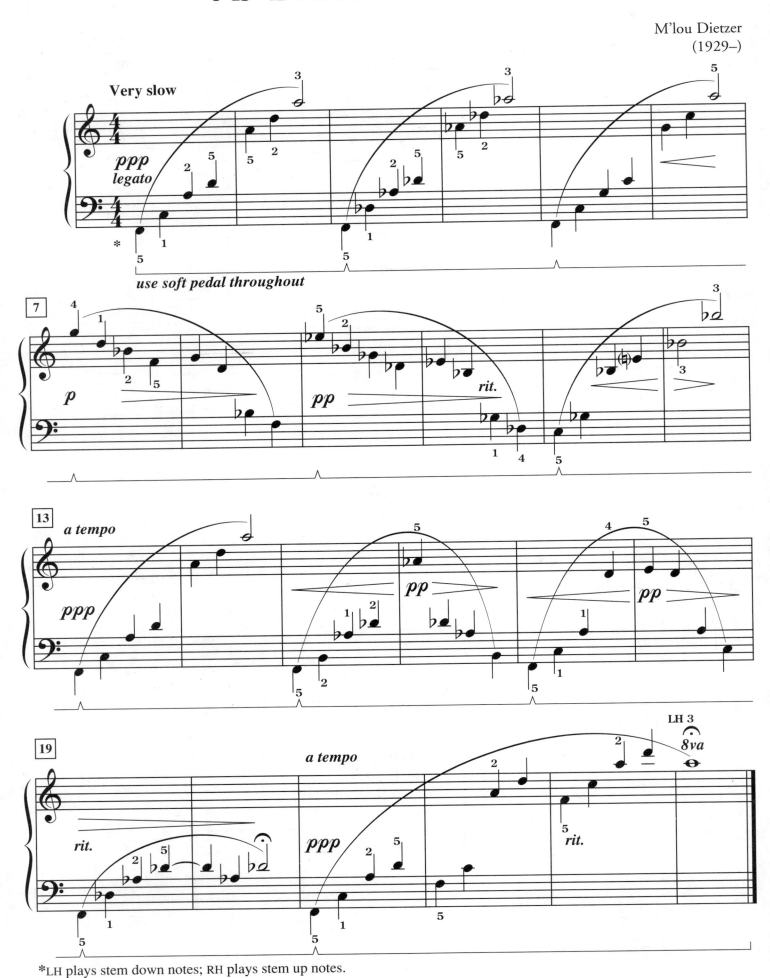

*LH plays stem down notes; RH plays stem up notes.